Lin

D0545503

Working?

discover libraries
**This book should be returned on or before
the due date.**

SC3

SC3	7/16		

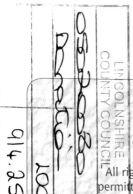

First published 2008
© George Keeping, 2008

COUNTRYSIDE BOOKS
3 Catherine Road
Newbury, Berkshire

To view our complete range of books,
please visit us at
www.countrysidebooks.co.uk

ISBN 978 1 84674 083 1

Photographs by the author
Maps by Gelder Design & Mapping

Designed by Peter Davies, Nautilus Design

Produced through MRM Associates Ltd, Reading
Typeset by CJWT Solutions, St Helens
Printed by Information Press, Oxford

All material for the manufacture of this book
was sourced from sustainable forests

Contents

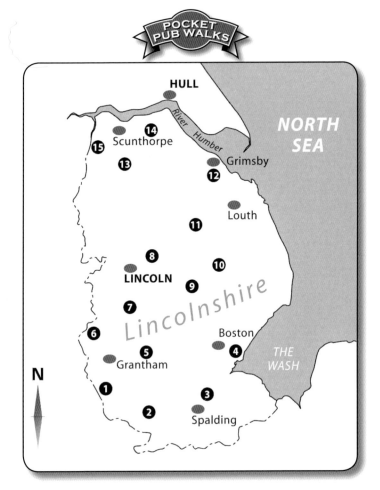

POCKET PUB WALKS

HULL

NORTH SEA

River Humber

Scunthorpe

⑮ ⑭

⑬

Grimsby

⑫

Louth

⑪

⑧

LINCOLN

⑩

⑨

Lincolnshire

⑦

⑥

Boston

⑤

④

THE WASH

Grantham

N

①

③

②

Spalding

Area map showing location of the walks

Introduction

Lincolnshire is a large county, and as such embraces a wide variety of countryside which includes the chalk uplands of the Wolds (designated as an Area of Outstanding Natural Beauty), the long escarpment of Lincoln Edge, rolling countryside around Grantham and, of course, the Fens. It certainly isn't all flat, as you will find when you explore the walks in this book. There is plenty to look at, on or near the walks – country houses, nature reserves, canals, wartime defences and the sites of castles and of lost villages. But it is probably the present-day villages that will give the greatest pleasure – many are still active communities with their shop, ancient church and, of course, pub. Try and support them if you can.

The walks themselves are all circular, starting and finishing at a pub, and vary in length from 2½ to 6½ miles. For each, you can get an idea of when the pub will be open and of the variety of food available. If you are planning to leave your car in the car park while you do the walk, please check at the pub first.

There is also information for each walk about the conditions underfoot and whether you can expect to encounter stiles on the way. Stout walking shoes or lightweight boots should be perfectly adequate for all paths, but some cross arable fields and will be muddy at times. Although there is a map for each walk, this is really to identify the points mentioned in the written directions and does not include much of the surrounding area. Ordnance Survey Explorer maps are the best way to get the most out of the walks – the necessary sheet numbers are given for each route.

Lincolnshire is excellent family walking country and I would like to dedicate this book to my own, who have shown remarkable patience as I have fumbled with maps, notes and cameras – the promise of a good meal goes a long way!

For my part, it has been a great pleasure to reacquaint myself with some of Lincolnshire's more far-flung footpaths – I hope you have as much fun walking these routes as I have had in researching them.

George Keeping

Publisher's Note

We hope that you obtain considerable enjoyment from this book; great care has been taken in its preparation. However, changes of landlord and actual closures are sadly not uncommon. Likewise, although at the time of publication all routes followed public rights of way or permitted paths, diversion orders can be made and permissions withdrawn.

We cannot, of course, be held responsible for such diversion orders and any inaccuracies in the text which result from these or any other changes to the routes nor any damage which might result from walkers trespassing on private property. We are anxious though that all details covering the walks are kept up to date and would therefore welcome information from readers which would be relevant to future editions.

The simple sketch maps that accompany the walks in this book are based on notes made by the author whilst checking out the routes on the ground. However, for the benefit of a proper map, we do recommend that you purchase the relevant Ordnance Survey sheet covering your walk. The Ordnance Survey maps are widely available, especially through booksellers and local newsagents.

1 Skillington

The Cross Swords Inn

Of all the walks featured in this book, this one is probably the easiest to follow, as the route takes hedged trackways and a minor country road. The walk starts in the charming stone village of Skillington, set in rolling countryside close to the border with Leicestershire, and for part of its course follows the county boundary. This is part of the ancient Sewstern Lane, an old cattle-droving route which is believed to have its origins in prehistoric times. The walk also passes close to the village church, which, uniquely for Lincolnshire, has a connection with the golden age of Victorian mountaineering.

THE PUB The **Cross Swords Inn** has been in existence from at least 1830 and it is likely that the site was occupied by an ale-

Lincolnshire

Distance – 3¼ miles

OS Explorer 247 Grantham. GR 898257
The walk runs entirely along green lanes and roadside verges. There are no stiles or other obstacles and the surface is generally good, but can be muddy.

Starting point The Cross Swords Inn, Skillington.

How to get there *Skillington lies about 2 miles west of the A1 – it is best to turn off at the B676 Colsterworth roundabout and head towards Stainby, before turning right to Skillington. The Cross Swords Inn stands on the left as you enter the village. There is parking beside the pub and nearby in The Square.*

house long before that. Today the Cross Swords is a very friendly village pub which also offers an extensive menu of home-cooked food that should appeal to all tastes. For starters you can choose from a range that includes wild mushrooms, a salad of marinated figs and pancetta with a honey and mustard dressing or black pudding with a red onion and apple marmalade. Main courses include chicken breast in creamy tarragon sauce and Gressingham duck. There is also a fish menu and a variety of vegetarian meals. At lunchtimes there is a carvery, but sandwiches and light snacks are also available. A traditional roast is served on Sunday. You can eat in a separate dining area, or in the bar with its roaring wintertime fire. Among the beers available are Tom Wood and Red MacGregor.

Opening times are Monday 7 pm to 11 pm; Tuesday and Wednesday 12 noon to 2 pm and 7 pm to 11 pm; Thursday, Friday and Saturday 12 noon to 2 pm and 5 pm to 11 pm; Sunday 12 noon to 5 pm.
☎ *01476 861132*

Skillington (Walk 1)

1 From the car park, turn left and left again, heading uphill, and take the exit from **The Square** into **Buckminster Lane** to the right of the Methodist chapel. Where **Stonepit Lane** branches off to the left, continue ahead onto the unsurfaced extension of **Buckminster Lane**. Descend towards the Cringle Brook and then carry on in the direction of a water tower on the skyline. Some distance before the tower, you come to a junction with another green lane.

2 Turn right onto this track, which is part of the ancient **Sewstern Lane** that for many miles marks the boundary between Lincolnshire and Leicestershire – it is also part of the Viking Way long-distance footpath. Follow the track as it winds its way northwards to meet **Sproxton Road**.

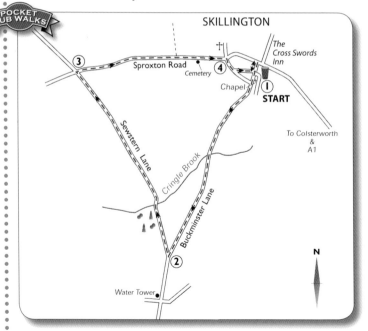

POCKET PUB WALKS

SKILLINGTON

Lincolnshire

Buckminster Lane

3 Follow the road to the right. Lincolnshire Wildlife Trust manages the verges for their conservation value as part of its Protected Roadside Verge scheme. At certain times of the year you may see miniature roller bales of hay, cut to keep down the level of nutrients and encourage the growth of meadow flowers. Carry on past the cemetery on the right and back to the edge of the village.

4 *If you wish to visit the church,* follow the road around to the left. In the late 19th century the vicar for the parish was Charles Hudson, the leading British mountaineer of his day, who along with three companions was tragically killed in 1865 on the way down after the first ascent of the Matterhorn. He is remembered in stained-glass windows and a display inside the church. *To continue*

the walk, turn into **Back Lane**, passing close to the site of the medieval Fish Well. After a small estate of modern houses, bear left into **Middle Street**, which takes you back to **The Square** and the **Cross Swords**.

Places of interest nearby

Woolsthorpe Manor at Woolsthorpe–by-Colsterworth, is a 17th-century manor house that was the birthplace and home of Sir Isaac Newton. It is now looked after by the National Trust. The orchard contains a descendant of the famous apple tree and there is a Science Discovery Centre, which explains the principles behind some of Newton's most famous discoveries. The entrance is on Water Lane and it is signposted from Colsterworth. The Manor is open from 1 pm to 5 pm on weekends between the beginning of March and the end of October and on Wednesday, Thursday and Friday from the beginning of April to the beginning of October. It is also open on Bank Holiday Mondays and on Good Friday. Check in advance for precise opening times and details of admission charges.
☎ *01476 860338*

Taking its name from the Norman French for 'beautiful view' (although the locals have defiantly pronounced it as 'beaver' for almost as long) **Belvoir Castle** has been the home of the Duke and Duchess of Rutland for a thousand years. The present castle dates from the early 19th century and, together with the surrounding grounds, is open to the public. There is an adventure playground and a restaurant. Opening times vary during the year, but the castle is open 11 am to 5 pm (4 pm on Saturday) on most days from May to August. The castle is signposted (and clearly visible) from the A52 west of Grantham.
☎ *01476 871000*

2 **Edenham**

The Five Bells

This walk starts in the delightful village of Edenham which rests within a bend of the East Glen River. This is Hereward the Wake country – the Saxon outlaw is supposed to have lived at nearby Bourne – and Charles Kingsley worked on his book about Hereward while staying at Edenham vicarage in 1886. The route takes you through the village and on into the popular Bourne Wood, with its own sculpture trail. Along the way there are good views of the surrounding countryside and of nearby Grimsthorpe Castle. The walk returns alongside the River Glen and past St Michael's church where you can see fragments of Anglo-Saxon sculpture inside.

Distance – 3½ miles

OS Explorer 248 Bourne & Heckington. GR 061218
Fairly easy walking on tracks and field-paths, but some paths in Bourne Wood can be muddy after rain. There are some stiles along the way.

Starting point The Five Bells in Edenham.

How to get there *Edenham and the Five Bells are on the A151, about 3 miles west of Bourne on the way to Corby Glen. Walkers may use the pub car park with permission.*

THE PUB Families will enjoy a visit to the **Five Bells** as it has a large beer garden with a children's play area and, if any energy is left over after the walk, the attraction of a bouncy castle. The pub itself dates from the 1880s and is built of local stone to match the style of the rest of the village. Inside it has the feel of a friendly local and serves a range of reasonably priced traditional pub food ranging from lunchtime snacks like sandwiches to full three-course meals. Specialities include steaks and a regular Sunday roast. There is a range of fine draught beers, including Sam Smith's.

Open all week 12 noon to 2.30 pm and 6.30 pm to 11 pm.
Food is served: all week 12 noon to 2 pm and 6.30 pm to 9 pm.
☎ *01778 591235*

1 Turn right out of the **Five Bells** car park and after a hundred yards go down **School Lane**, which you follow past the school and the entrance to **Church Lane**. At the edge of the village, at a sharp left-hand bend, carry straight on up the hill on a minor road. As you climb the hill you will pass a pond, which is a good

place to turn back for a view of the church, village and, in the distance, **Grimsthorpe Castle**.

2 Cross the cattle grid just past **Scoth Farm Cottages** and where the tarmac bends to the left, carry straight on along a stone track. The track heads towards a gap in the hedge, but do not pass through. Continue instead down the grass field keeping the hedge on your right and go through a gate onto a path that leads to the edge of **Bourne Wood**.

3 Continue in the same direction inside the wood for a few yards, before bearing left onto a wider grass path. Follow this until, shortly after crossing a small stream, you come to a crossroads with a broad stone track. Turn right onto the track, which is one of the main routes through Bourne Wood and can be popular with walkers and cyclists at weekends, and follow it for just over

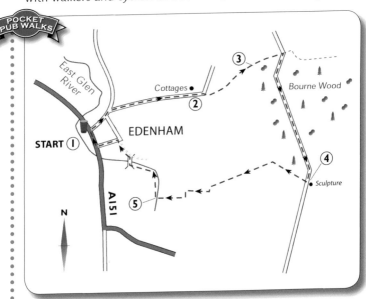

On the track through Bourne Wood

½ mile. Soon after descending a steep slope the track takes a sharp bend to the right and after a little way is crossed by another track marked with the familiar yellow arrows of a public footpath. The crossing point is easily identified by a bench and a low pillar (part of the wood's Sculpture Trail) that appears to depict scenes from Hereward's struggle against the Norman invaders.

4 Turn right onto the footpath and follow it until a bridge takes you out of **Bourne Wood** and onto a field-edge path alongside the trees. The woodland is left behind as the path reaches the brow of the hill. The waymarks lead you to the left around the

edge of a field before you start downhill with the hedge to your left. About halfway down, the path swaps to the other side of the hedge and runs on to cross the river by a wide concrete bridge.

5 Turn right at the fingerpost immediately after crossing the bridge and walk alongside the river, before bending to the left and passing the sewage treatment works. Cross the river by a narrow bridge and walk a few yards across a pasture field to meet a concrete track, where a left turn along it leads back to **Church Lane** beside an attractive old cottage. A left turn along the road leads you back to the A151, where a right turn beside an enormous cedar soon brings the pub car park back into sight.

Places of interest nearby

Two miles north-west of Edenham lies **Grimsthorpe Castle**, a magnificent house partly rebuilt by Vanbrugh in 1722, which is still the family seat of the Willoughby de Eresby family. The house, park and gardens are open to the public from April to September, generally on Sundays, Thursdays and Bank Holiday Mondays and more often during the summer months. There are cycle routes through the extensive parkland and an adventure playground.
☎ 01778 591205 www.grimsthorpe.co.uk

Approximately the same distance to the south-east is the market town of **Bourne**, which has a good range of shops. Worth a visit is the **Heritage Centre**, housed in historic Baldock's watermill. The Heritage Centre is open at weekends from 2 pm until 4 pm, and contains local history displays and a permanent exhibition about the famous local racing driver Raymond Mays and the story of ERA and BRM racing cars.
☎ 01778 422775 www.bournecivicsociety.org.uk

3 Pinchbeck

The Ship Inn

Watercourses through the Fens around Spalding are generally broad and straight, but this walk bucks the trend and follows a length of the River Glen that retains a more natural sinuous course. In springtime the surrounding countryside is a riot of colour as the daffodils and tulips, grown hereabouts as commercial crops, come into bloom. The walk skirts around the northern edge of Pinchbeck, a large village with a range of shops and a church with a fine Perpendicular tower,

Distance – 2½ miles

OS Explorer 249 Spalding & Holbeach. GR 234260
The walk follows minor roads and generally level riverside
paths. There are no stiles.

Starting point The Ship Inn at Pinchbeck.

How to get there *Pinchbeck lies 1 mile to the west of the
A16 Boston to Stamford road, some 2 miles north of Spalding.
Follow the B1356 into the centre of the village and then turn
along the B1180, marked to West Pinchbeck and Bourne. The
Ship lies on the right, immediately after a humpbacked railway
bridge. For those using the pub, there is a car park.*

and passes close to two other towers – the dominating water
tower, built in 1954, and an old windmill dating from 1848.

THE PUB

If you like sitting and watching the river flow by, then the
Ship Inn is the place to visit. The 400-year-old pub is right
next to the River Glen and for those long summer evenings
there are riverside picnic tables and a play area. The Ship,
with its quaint thatched roof, looks tiny from the outside
– but inside there is plenty of room, with a comfortable bar
(serving Speckled Hen and Greene King IPA) and adjacent pool
area, while to one side there is a large dining room extension,
home to the Plum Restaurant. The menu gives plenty of choice
for both lunch and evening meals. Starters include goat's cheese
and onion tartlet, tiger prawns and Camembert in a box with
rustic bread. On the main menu are pork chop with caramelised
fruits and mashed potato, beef in Stilton sauce, spicy chilli beef
strips with spiced beans and Cajun wedges and more traditional
favourites such as sausage and mash; all main courses come with
a selection of vegetables. There is also a full children's menu.

Open all week from 12 noon to midnight. Food is served when the pub is open.
☎ *01775 723792*

1 Turn right out of the car park and cross over the bridge, before turning left along a footpath running beside the Glen. The path rejoins the road at a gate, where a right turn takes you to a T-junction. Head to the left, along **North Gate** and past the old windmill until you turn into **Old Fen Lane**.

2 **Old Fen Lane** soon becomes a quiet narrow road winding between the Fenland fields. At the next road junction turn right again and after ¼ mile, beyond a sharp right bend, turn into

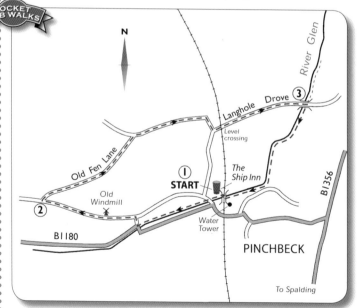

The water tower passed near the end of the walk

Langhole Drove. This takes you over the Sleaford to Spalding railway line at the Flax Mill level crossing and then on to cross the River Glen once more.

3 Once over the bridge turn right onto a footpath (narrow at first) that follows the river. The path soon climbs onto the bank above the river, giving wider views over the surrounding countryside. You skirt around houses on the edge of **Pinchbeck**, before

passing close to the water tower and meeting the railway once more, just to the left of the bridge over the river. Cross the tracks with care and on the far side enter straight into the grounds of the pub, walking alongside a row of picnic tables set under riverside willows.

Places of interest nearby

The attractions at **Springfields** are certain to provide something to suit every taste. There is a complex of 43 outlet stores, with bargains on anything from fashion to home items, and the renowned 25-acre Festival Gardens, which include celebrity showcase gardens, a large garden centre and a children's indoor play area. Springfields is also home to the Fens Discovery Centre, with displays charting the history and traditions of the area. There is a choice of cafés on the site. Open: Monday to Friday 10 am to 6 pm, Saturday 9 am to 6 pm and Sunday 11 am to 5 pm. Public holidays: 10 am to 6 pm. Springfields is signposted from the A16 Spalding bypass.
☎ *01775 724843*

The **Pinchbeck Engine** is a restored steam-powered beam engine of a type that was once common hereabouts. Every year, from the time it was built in 1833 until it was replaced with an electric pump in 1952, the engine did its bit to keep the Fens drained by lifting an average of three million tons of water at a rate of 7,500 gallons per minute. The engine, which can be turned electrically for demonstrations, forms part of a small museum and is open daily from 10 am to 4 pm from April to October. Admission is free and there is a car park, picnic site and toilet. The site is signposted from the A16, immediately north of the roundabout with the A151.
☎ *01775 725861.*

4 **Freiston**

The Castle Inn

You are never far away from water in this part of Lincolnshire, and the parish of Freiston is positioned between that key to the Fenland drainage system, the Hobhole Drain, and the waters of the Wash. In the intensively farmed landscape of the Fens, the banks of the larger drains provide a refuge for wildlife and some lengths are actively managed as nature reserves. This walk takes in part of the

Distance – 3 miles

OS Explorer 261 Boston. GR 369451
A gentle walk following the banks of the Hobhole Drain and quiet country roads and tracks. The surface is uneven in places, but there are no stiles to negotiate.

Starting point The Castle Inn at Haltoft End, Freiston.

How to get there The Castle Inn stands next to the A52 Skegness road, some 2 miles east of Boston. If you are using the pub, you can park in the car park. Otherwise there is kerbside parking in Oak House Lane, adjacent to the pub.

western bank of the Hobhole Drain and returns through the village of Freiston and its surrounding farmland.

THE PUB

The **Castle Inn**, with the cream and red colour scheme of the local Batemans brewery, stands beside the road between Boston and Skegness – one of a series of pubs along the road providing refreshment for people on their way in search of sand, sea and sunshine. In fact the Castle is surprisingly homely inside, with a double bay-windowed main bar that maintains the seaside theme with models of sailing boats and carvings of sea birds – the walls are decorated with paintings by local artists. Outside there is a garden, a covered seating area and swings for younger visitors. The welcome is warm and there is a varied menu with a special-price lunchtime menu that includes dessert. Portions are enough for the healthiest appetite. The range includes traditional favourites such as liver and bacon, steak and ale pie, a range of fish and seafood under 'Fisherman's choice' and a selection of vegetarian options. Friday night is a special fish night and there is a popular traditional Sunday roast, with a choice of beef, lamb or chicken.

*Open on Tuesday to Saturday 11 am to 2.30 pm and 5 pm
to 11 pm, and on Sunday 12 noon to 10.30 pm. Open in the
evening on Monday 5 pm to 11 pm. Food is served on Tuesday
to Saturday 11.30 am to 2 pm and (including Monday) 5 pm
to 8 pm, but on Sunday 12 noon to 8 pm.*
☎ *01205 760393*

1 Set off to the right out of the car park and soon after turn right
down **Oak House Lane**. The road bends to the left and comes
alongside the **Hobhole Bank**, where you follow a footpath off

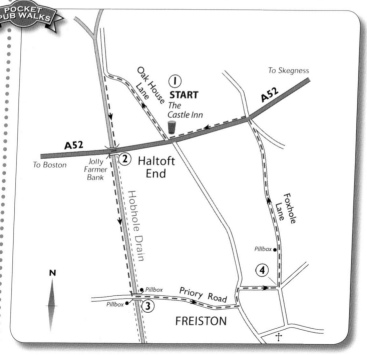

Foxhole Lane

to the left along the drain side. The path runs along the edge of fields, with views to the west of two local landmarks – Boston Stump and the blue-grey block of the Pilgrim Hospital. Shortly after entering a more wooded area, the path narrows to pass beside some buildings before coming out onto the main A52 beside **Haltoft End Bridge**.

2 Cross the road with caution and go over the bridge before turning left down the footpath along **Jolly Farmer Bank** – a wide grassy strip along the western side of the Hobhole Drain. The path soon narrows and winds between gnarled trees along a terrace between the drain and the base of the bank – a delightful stretch that seems a million miles away from the relentless agriculture of the surrounding Fens. Over to the left you get occasional glimpses of the village of **Freiston** with its square-towered church.

3 The path emerges onto **Priory Road** where you turn left and cross **Freiston Bridge** (to get a good view of the bridge's handsome brick arches, follow the path along the eastern side of the drain for a few yards). Beside the bridge are two old pillboxes and as you look along the Hobhole Drain it is easy to appreciate the strategic importance of the few crossing points over the broad watercourses hereabouts. To continue the walk, follow the road for ½ mile to the centre of Freiston. Turn left onto **Church Road** and, opposite the **Kings Head** (which also serves food), turn right down **Park Lane**. There are playing fields on the right and, further on, a play area.

4 Turn left at the T-junction onto **Butterwick Road** and almost immediately bear left onto **Foxhole Lane**, a pleasant Fenland roadway complete with its own pillbox, which curves northwards between the fields back towards the A52. Once more cross the main road carefully and turn left along the footway back in the direction of the prominent roofline of the **Castle Inn**.

Place of interest nearby

Maud Foster Windmill is a working mill dating from 1819 – with seven floors it is one of the tallest in the country. There is a tearoom and shop, which sells organic flour, porridge oats, local history books and souvenirs. The mill stands close to Boston town centre. There is a free car park. Open all year: Wednesday 10 am to 5 pm, Saturday 11 am to 5 pm, Sunday 12 noon to 5 pm. Extra days in July and August – Thursday 11 am to 5 pm and Friday 11 am to 5 pm. Bank holidays – 10 am to 5 pm. Christmas and New Year period – closed.
☎ *01205 352188*

5 Oasby

The Houblon Inn

This walk samples the rolling uplands that lie on either side of Grantham and contain some of the most delightful villages in all Lincolnshire: solid limestone cottages, many with red tiled roofs, gathered round churches. In the past the landscape, together with good access along the Great North Road, made this area a popular location for country houses. The walk explores the area around the village of Oasby and passes through the landscaped grounds of Culverthorpe Hall.

THE
PUB

The **Houblon Inn** takes its name from a local landowner, Sir John Houblon, who from 1694 to 1697 was the first governor of the Bank of England – Sir John's portrait appears on the modern £50 note. The building is over 350 years old

Distance – 3½ miles

OS Explorer 248 Bourne & Heckington. GR 003391
A varied walk on footpaths and quiet roads. The route crosses a number of grass fields fenced for horses or stock and there are some stiles to negotiate.

Starting point The Houblon Inn at Oasby.

How to get there *Oasby is signposted about 2½ miles east of the B6403 between Grantham and Ancaster. Turn left as you enter the village and follow the road round to the Houblon Inn. If you are visiting the pub, there is a small car park at the back – otherwise you can park with consideration in the village.*

which is reflected in the low beams and stone floors of both the main bar and restaurant. The large open fire makes the pub a welcome haven after a bracing winter walk and there is a fine selection of beers: the resident 'Tiger' from Everards and up to four guest ales (including on occasion the Grantham-brewed High Dyke – the local name for the Roman Ermine Street that bisects Lincolnshire). There are varied menus for starters, main courses and puddings on blackboards in the bar. Examples of lunchtime fare are: chicken and cream sauce with almond and mixed leaves, mushroom and walnut risotto and the old favourite of sausage and mash. There are also lighter meals, including soup, sandwiches and scrambled egg bagels.

Open Tuesday to Saturday 12 noon to 3.30 pm and 6.30 pm to 11 pm; Sunday 12 noon to 4 pm and 7 pm to 10.30 pm. Closed on Monday. Food is served when the pub is open, except on Sunday evening.
☎ *01529 455215*

1 Turn left out of the pub car park and follow the road until, on a sharp bend, a footpath heads off to the left beside **Corner Cottage**. A stile leads into a paddock and from there the footpath goes diagonally to the left across to the far corner, where a gate leads into the next field. Continue on the same line across the next two fields until a gap in the hedge gives access to a stile and footbridge. From here take the signposted footpath straight ahead over the field to reach a road.

2 Cross onto the road signposted to Kelby and in less than ½ mile, turn right onto a bridleway. Shortly after a junction with a footpath, the bridleway passes through a hedge and turns sharply to the left. After about 200 yards it turns to the right and follows a broad grass track towards the buildings of **Park Farm**.

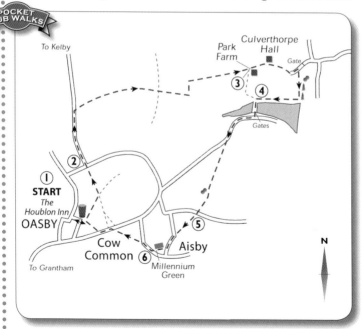

Lincolnshire

Culverthorpe Hall

[3] At the farm, turn left and then bear to the right onto a drive that passes in front of **Culverthorpe Hall**. Continue along the drive and shortly before you come to the gates out of the park, turn right onto a waymarked route which descends past a small wood. Just before the edge of the lake, turn onto a narrow path between metal fences that heads off to the right parallel to the edge of the lake. This ends at a gate onto a surfaced track.

[4] Turn left and go on to circumvent the ornate gates to the left. Turn right along the road and follow it until, on a bend, a footpath is signposted leading off to the left. Head uphill diagonally across the field, aiming for a clump of trees on the skyline. As you climb, the views begin to widen and far away to the left you may glimpse the prominent tower of Boston Stump – a full 20 miles off. Pass the trees and continue across the next field to reach a road beside a prominent fingerpost.

[5] The path continues on the other side of the road and crosses the next field to a signposted gap in the hedge beside some

old agricultural machinery. Turn left along the road and just after the 30 mph sign at the entrance to **Aisby**, veer right and walk across the Millennium Green in front of a row of pleasant cottages, passing beside a hedged play area.

6 At the road on the far side of the Green, turn right for a few hundred yards until a signposted footpath leads off to the left across **Cow Common**. Turn left at the road and then take the third footpath off to the right – this leads you back to the path beside **Corner Cottage**, and so back to the **Houblon Inn**.

Places of interest nearby

Belton House, now in the care of the National Trust, is one of the finest examples of Restoration country house architecture and has featured in films such as the BBC's *Pride and Prejudice*. The grounds cover some 36 acres and include Italian and Dutch gardens, an orangery, a children's adventure playground (complete with railway) and a café. Belton is signposted from the A607 some 3 miles north of Grantham. The house is open on Wednesday to Sunday 12.30 pm to 5 pm from mid-March to late October. The garden and park are open on Wednesday to Sunday for most of the year and also on Monday and Tuesday in August. There is an admission charge.
☎ *01476 566116*

Nearby **Sleaford** is home to **The Hub** – the National Centre for Craft and Design, located in a recently converted seed warehouse in the town centre. The Hub has an ever-changing programme of activities, exhibitions and events, and there is also a café and craft shop. Opening hours are Monday to Sunday 10 am to 5 pm, bank holidays 10 am to 5 pm. Admission is free.
☎ *01529 308710*

6 **Dry Doddington**

The Wheatsheaf Inn

The village of **Dry Doddington** lives up to its name and sits high and dry on a hill above the broad curve of the River Witham. This means that for much of its length this walk enjoys sweeping views – westwards towards Nottingham and the Trent and northwards, almost 20 miles, towards Lincoln. The walk starts delightfully with the pub and church facing each other across the open space of the village green and then goes on, along a series of green lanes, to visit the neighbouring village of Claypole. The churches of Claypole and Dry Doddington both have distinctive profiles which provide reassuring help with navigation. The tower at Doddington is also one of a select group in Lincolnshire that leans at an alarming angle.

THE PUB Church, pub and village green – the quintessential English combination – but the **Wheatsheaf Inn** is also a top-class restaurant. The bar is stone flagged, with panelled benches and an open fire in winter, while the candlelit main dining

Distance – 4½ miles

OS Explorer 271 Newark-on-Trent. GR 849465
A walk along green lanes that returns on paths close to the River Witham. There are some stiles and paths across arable land may at times be muddy.

Starting point The Wheatsheaf Inn at Dry Doddington.

How to get there Dry Doddington lies 1½ miles east of the A1, 6 miles to the south of Newark. There is parking beside the green, opposite the pub.

room is all whitewashed stone walls and beams – parts of the building are said to date from the 14th century. Beer drinkers will be pleased to see Abbot Ale, Black Sheep and Tom Wood among the selection, while the menu includes wild mushroom and spinach risotto, slow-roast belly of pork, chargrilled Lincolnshire rump steak – and wonderful fish and chips. Pheasant, lobster and sea bass may be among the specials.

Open Tuesday and Wednesday 5 pm to 11 pm, Thursday to Saturday 12 noon to 2.30 pm (3 pm on Saturday) and 5 pm to 11 pm (6 pm to 11 pm on Saturday), Sunday 12 noon to 9.30 pm. Closed Monday. Food is served from 12 noon to 2 pm and 6 pm to 9.30 pm.
☎ *01400 281458*

1 Start off along **Main Street**, passing the church with its Norman doorway and leaning tower. Cross the end of **Claypole Lane** and then turn left 100 yards or so later onto a public footpath down **Green Lane**. At the end, turn right onto another path and follow waymarks straight ahead that lead to a path junction.

2 Turn left onto a bridleway, which rises gently giving wide views over to the neighbouring village of Claypole (our target on this walk) and beyond that to the course of the Trent valley with its power stations. The track leads on to a mobile phone mast, beyond which a path continues to cross a railway bridge over the East Coast main line. Follow the hedge line for about 100 yards beyond the bridge to a fingerpost.

3 Turn left onto the route marked as a 'restricted byway'. If the route is not clear, aim for a stile in the fence to the left of, and

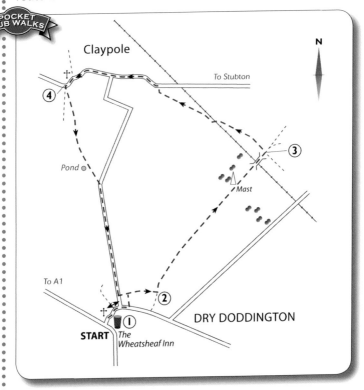

a little beyond, a prominent oak tree. Carry on in the same direction with the grassy bank of an old field boundary on your right, aiming for the spire of **Claypole church**. You cross another stile and then ascend a grassy track to a level crossing. Be extremely careful crossing the railway and at times of poor visibility make use of the telephone provided. On the far side, a lane leads to **Main Street**, which you follow to the left, through the village, until you reach **St Peter's church**. Shortly after, on a sharp right bend, leave the road where two footpaths are signposted heading off southwards.

4 Cross a paddock by two stiles and then cross the next arable field diagonally to the left, heading towards the distinctive silhouette of **Dry Doddington church** – a course which takes you past an electricity pole in the middle of the field to a waymark post in the far corner. Keep on the same line to a footbridge and then aim to the left of a group of trees beside a small pond. The path continues in the same direction to reach the Claypole to Dry Doddington road, where you turn right and follow the wide verge back to the village. At the T-junction turn right into **Main Street**, back to the pub.

Place of interest nearby

Newark Air Museum houses a wide range of aircraft, many of national significance, together with a varied display of aviation artefacts and engines. The museum is located on part of a former Second World War airfield two miles north-east of Newark-on-Trent at the Winthorpe Showground. It has a café and car parking and is open every day except Christmas Eve, Christmas Day, Boxing Day and New Year's Day. March to October 10 am to 5 pm, November to February 10 am to 4 pm.
☎ 01636 707170

The Joiners Arms

The landscape of Lincolnshire is dominated by the Lincoln Edge – a limestone escarpment that runs for most of the length of the county from the Humber to Grantham. This walk, although short, covers varied ground. It starts by climbing to take in part of the Edge (also known as the Cliff), looking down on the red roofs of the village of Welbourn, and then drops back to pass through the village itself. On the way it acquires a military flavour – passing the site of a small medieval castle and the birthplace of the first soldier ever to have risen all the way through the ranks from Private to Field Marshal. There is also the chance to lengthen the walk slightly to visit Welbourn church with its strange irregular spire.

Distance – 2½ miles

OS Explorer 272 Lincoln. GR 964540
There is one climb on the walk and, as the route follows the spring line above the village, there can be muddy patches after rain. There is only one stile on the walk.

Starting point The Joiners Arms, High Street, Welbourn.

How to get there *The village of Welbourn lies just off the A607 Grantham to Lincoln road, between the villages of Wellingore and Leadenham. Turn off the main road into Hall Lane, bear right then left at the green and follow the road into High Street, where the pub stands on the left.*

THE PUB

The **Joiners Arms** may look like a typical village pub from the outside, but if reports in the local press are to be believed, there is more to it than meets the eye. The pub has origins going back to the 18th century and in recent years there have been tales of supernatural pranks being played by a ghost that, strange to say, appears to enjoy listening to Robbie Williams. None of this deters the locals and it is clear from the display of trophies that the pub is at the heart of Welbourn's social life. There is a long panelled main bar, serving a selection of real ales and flanked by tables from which you can look out and reflect on the pace of village life. At the weekends the pub serves traditional bar meals, with a choice that includes pizza, burgers, pies and chips.

Open Sunday 12 noon to 12 midnight, Monday and Tuesday 4.30 pm to 12 midnight, Wednesday, Thursday and Friday 12 noon to 2 pm and 4.30 pm to 12 midnight, Saturday 11.30 am to 12 midnight. Food served at weekends only: 12 noon to 2 pm and 6 pm to closing. ☎ *01400 272430*

1 Follow **High Street** to the right from the car park and turn left at the end, opposite the old forge. At the green, with its large horse chestnut tree, go right, passing a row of cottages with a memorial to Sir William Robertson, who rose from 'Trooper to Field Marshal'. Bear right onto a road signposted to **Brant Broughton** and, where the road bends to the right, go straight ahead onto a footpath, which leads by a kissing gate into a grass field. Carry on ahead across the field until a second kissing gate leads into a lay-by next to the A607. Walk to the right and at the end of the lay-by cross the road with care and set off along a footpath marked with North Kesteven District Council's 'Stepping Out' logo.

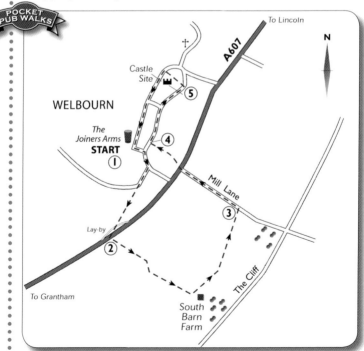

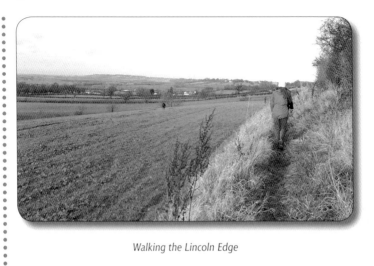

Walking the Lincoln Edge

[2] The path runs to the right of a hedgerow and begins to climb, giving views to the north towards the neighbouring village of **Wellingore**. At the top of the slope, turn left onto a waymarked path in front of the buildings, which passes to the left of some trees and then follows the edge of a field as it runs northwards along **the Cliff**. The village of **Welbourn** is below you to the left and beyond that the steaming cooling towers of power stations mark the line of the **River Trent**.

[3] The path leads on to **Mill Lane**, where you turn left downhill and back to the A607. Once again, cross the road with care and take a footpath that enters a grass field, through a kissing gate. Cross the field to a hidden stile that leads to a narrow enclosed path, which emerges onto **Beck Street**.

[4] Turn right and continue past the well-stocked post office and shop to a point opposite the village hall pond, where you pass through a gate on the left into a sloping field. This is the site of **Welbourn castle**, whose history is recounted on information boards.

Lincolnshire

5 Cross to a bench at the highest point on the far side of the field. Just to the right of the bench, steps lead down to a bridge over the stream that doubled as the castle moat. Cross over onto **Castle Hill**. *A right turn here* can take you to St Chad's church where you can find interesting graffiti in the porch, a memorial to Field Marshal Robertson and a fearsome gargoyle. As you were looking down on the church earlier from the Cliff you will probably have noticed that the sides of the spire are not straight, but curved (whether through accident or design) to give it a distinct humped profile. *If you are not visiting the church*, turn left. **Castle Hill** becomes **High Street** shortly before the Wesleyan chapel and in no time you are back beside the **Joiners Arms**.

Places of interest nearby

Fulbeck Manor Stables Craft Centre stands close to the A607 in the village of Fulbeck, 4 miles south of Welbourn. It includes a saddler's workshop, papercraft artist and galleries displaying a wide variety of art and craft made locally and nationally. There is a tearoom and free car parking. Opening times are Tuesday to Sunday and bank holidays 10.30 am to 4.30 pm.
☎ *01400 273724*

About 3 miles east of Welbourn, on the road linking the village to the A15, stands the 12th-century **tower of the preceptory of the Knights Templar**, the military order formed to guard pilgrims and guard the shrines of the Holy Land. The tower, all that remains of the characteristic circular Templar church, is open to the public during daylight hours. There is free parking on site, but no other facilities. For further information contact the Sleaford Tourist Information Centre.
☎ *01529 414294*

8 **Fiskerton**

The Carpenters Arms

The village of Fiskerton provides a delightful walk that explores a network of narrow green lanes and riverside paths. The centrepiece is the River Witham whose raised banks carry water through the Fens at a level that overtops the roofs of nearby houses. The river has not always been so well controlled – in centuries past this was a wild and watery area. Archaeological finds from the river show that people have lived around Fiskerton since prehistoric times. The remains have been

Lincolnshire

Distance – 4½ miles

OS Explorer 272 Lincoln. GR 049720
Terrain Easy walking on field and riverside paths and green lanes. There are some stiles.

Starting point The Carpenters Arms in Fiskerton.

How to get there *Fiskerton is close to the River Witham, on the minor road to Bardney some 5 miles east of Lincoln. The road from Lincoln comes into the village past the Carpenters Arms. Walkers may use the pub car park with permission.*

found of a wooden causeway that stretched almost 200 yards into the marsh alongside the river, together with log boats and ritually destroyed weapons. Although there is no part of the walk higher than 45 ft above sea level, the views are far-reaching: in one direction the silhouette of Lincoln Minster and in the other the broad tops of the Wolds, more than 16 miles away.

THE PUB

As well as being a centre for village social life, the **Carpenters Arms** is also well known for its delicious home-cooked food. The pub is a free house with a large main bar that serves Batemans and Everards ales. The cosy lounge bar, decorated with pictures of Second World War aircraft (a reminder of the nearby wartime airfield) opens through brick arches into the large restaurant extension. The main menu includes chicken, onion and Stilton pie, pork loin encased in sage and onion stuffing and a cold meat platter, but there are also vegetarian and fish menus. For those wanting a lighter meal, there is a separate snack menu that features a selection of bagels and jacket potatoes and the ever-popular ploughman's lunch. The sweet-toothed can indulge in a formidable selection of desserts. For sunny days there is a beer garden at the rear of the pub.

Open Monday 6 pm to 11 pm, Tuesday to Saturday 12 noon to 2.30 pm and 6 pm to 11 pm, Sunday 12 noon to 3 pm and 7 pm to 10.30 pm. Meals are served Tuesday to Saturday 12 noon to 2 pm and 6 pm to 8.30 pm, Sunday 12 noon to 2.30 pm. No food is served on Monday.
☎ *01522 751806*

1 From the pub car park, turn left until the road bends sharply to the right, where you need to turn into **Nelson Road** next to the post office. After 100 yards a narrow waymarked path leads off to the right next to 'Shetlands'. Cross a footbridge and turn right along the edge of the field, until after a second bridge you can climb onto the bank of the Witham. A left turn here leads on to the prominent steel structure of **Five Mile Bridge**, which has

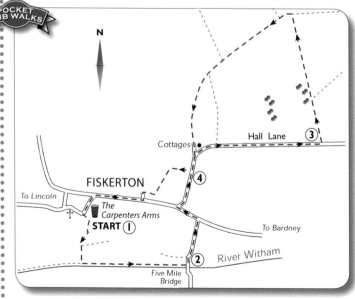

Beside the River Witham

recently been converted to give ramped access over the river to the Water Rail Way, part of the National Cycle Network.

2 Don't cross the bridge, but turn left onto a narrow lane that takes you to the main road. Take care when crossing the road and follow the footway to the left until you can turn right into **Hall Lane**. As you walk along the lane the views to the left begin to open out towards the Wolds. On the horizon are two prominent masts: Belmont (TV) and Stenigot Pylon (a Second World War radar station, see Walk 11). After a mile the track bends sharply to the left and acquires a concrete surface.

3 Turn left, continue along the track and then, shortly after a right-hand bend, take a signposted bridleway that runs off to the left next to a small wood. The path runs uphill along the edge of a

field to meet another bridleway, hedged on both sides, where you turn left once more. This narrow lane soon gives way to a field-edge path, alongside a hedge which, if your timing is right, is laden with wild plums. Continue on, ignoring other paths signposted on either side, until you emerge onto **Hall Lane** next to some cottages.

4 After just 100 yards take a footpath on the right over a stile to cross a grass field. Carry on through a hand gate and then follow the path as it bears left across a field and begins to run gently downhill. At the edge of the field the path turns sharply right to run behind a row of houses, before turning left down an estate road to the main road. Turn right along the road, past a shop and the village green, until the road bears left into **High Street** and runs back to the **Carpenters Arms**.

Place of interest nearby

There is, of course, plenty to see in nearby **Lincoln**, but one of the newer attractions is **The Collection**, an award-winning museum which sits next to the Usher Art Gallery close to Steep Hill in the lower part of the city. The Collection includes a wealth of artefacts from the Stone Age through to the medieval period – including a reconstruction of part of the Fiskerton causeway. The Collection also has a temporary exhibition programme; there is a shop and café. Admission is free, but there may be an admission charge to some temporary exhibitions. Open 10 am to 5 pm seven days a week – last admission 4.30 pm. Closed Christmas Eve, Christmas Day, Boxing Day, New Year's Eve and New Year's Day. The Collection is on Danes Terrace and is signposted from the city centre.
☎ *01522 550990*

The Ebrington Arms

This short walk takes in a length of the River Bain that was transformed by the canal engineers to form part of the Horncastle Navigation which opened in 1802. The canal is now derelict and its banks, together with the adjacent 'natural' line of the Old River Bain, give an elevated walk through grassland. Kirkby on Bain, with its mixture of traditional and modern houses, sits astride the back road from Tattershall to Horncastle. Its setting, in the gravel-rich valley, is admirable and it has a traditional village pub to add to its charms. The walk can be extended slightly to link to the adjacent village of Roughton, whose church has an unusual brick tower.

Distance – 3 or 3½ miles

OS Explorer 273 Lincolnshire Wolds South. GR 240627
Easy walking alongside a former canal. The paths are
mostly across grassland and there are some stiles.

Starting point The Ebrington Arms at Kirkby on Bain.

How to get there *Kirkby on Bain lies 1 mile west of the A153,
midway between Coningsby and Horncastle. Turn westwards
off the main road south of Haltham and then left after the
bridge over the Bain. The Ebrington Arms stands on the edge
of the village and there is a car park that you can use if you are
visiting the pub.*

THE PUB The **Ebrington Arms** is a delightful combination of village
pub and restaurant, with good home cooking and a wide
range of real ales that includes Greene King, Batemans and
Marston's. The beams in the bar are covered with unusual beer
mats and old pennies. The same menu covers the bar and the
restaurant – and there is a great deal of choice. To start you can
try prawns in Marie Rose sauce or goat's cheese and honey and for
a main course braised steak with Ebrington Ale or roast Norfolk
duckling. On fine days you can sit in the adjacent beer garden
and play area and there is seating in front of the pub too.

*Open Monday 6 pm to 11 pm and Tuesday to Sunday 12 noon
to 2.30 pm and 6 pm to 11 pm. Food is served Tuesday to
Sunday 12 noon to 2 pm and 6 pm to 9 pm.*
☎ *01526 354560*

1 From the car park, turn left down the road and, after about 200
yards where the road bends, take the first footpath signed off

to the left. Follow the track over the river, passing in front of a house and through a kissing gate into a grass field. Turn left and after a while climb onto the bank of the old **Horncastle Canal**. After about ½ mile a stile leads onto the road at **Red Mill Bridge**. Cross the road and continue along the bank, over a couple of stiles, until you reach a footbridge at the site of **Haltham Lock**.

2 Follow the raised embankment of the canal, which along this stretch still holds a respectable depth of water. The canal makes its way through pleasant grassland on both sides and the village

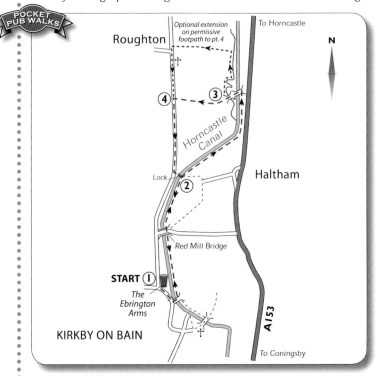

POCKET PUB WALKS

Roughton

Optional extension
on permissive
footpath to pt. 4

To Horncastle

N

④ ③

Horncastle Canal

Lock ②

Haltham

Red Mill Bridge

START ①

The
Ebrington
Arms

KIRKBY ON BAIN

A153

To Coningsby

The Horncastle Canal

of **Roughton** can be seen occupying a position on higher ground to the left. Keep to the bank as the canal bends to the left and after a while a substantial footbridge comes into sight. Cross this bridge and bear left across the field to go over a second smaller bridge.

3 *At this point a permissive path*, set out as part of the Countryside Stewardship scheme, provides the opportunity to lengthen the walk by continuing northwards along the **Old River Bain** and turning west to visit the village of **Roughton**. The route is waymarked along its length with white arrows and there is a map beside the bridge. Once in Roughton you can walk along the road southwards to rejoin the route at point 4. *For the main walk*, carry on ahead after the second bridge, over two stiles and then follow the edge of a field, until the path cuts across to exit onto the Roughton road beside a fingerpost.

4 Follow the wide roadside verge to the left and where the road bends to the right, a signposted footpath strikes off to the left

and climbs back onto the bank of the canal at **Haltham Lock**. Cross the concrete footbridge and turn right to retrace the route via **Red Mill Bridge** to the **Ebrington Arms**.

Places of interest nearby

The 15th-century, red-brick tower of **Tattershall Castle** rises to six floors and gives fantastic views over the surrounding countryside – binoculars are essential for any visit. There is a National Trust shop that also sells drinks, ice creams, etc. Nearby is a row of medieval almshouses and the cavernous Holy Trinity church. Open at weekends from 12 noon to 4 pm during March, November and early December and in addition on Monday, Tuesday, and Wednesday from 11 am to 5.30 pm from late March to mid-September. Car parking is free, but there is an admission charge for the castle. The car park is signposted to the right off the A153 Sleaford to Horncastle road as you enter the village.

☎ *01526 342543*

For over fifty years now the roar of the engines has caused Lincolnshire residents to look up as veteran Second World War aircraft fly to air shows around the country. Since 1986 it has been possible to see the aircraft at the **Battle of Britain Memorial Flight Visitor Centre** at RAF Coningsby. There is an exhibition centre and shop and guided tours to take you around the BBMF hanger. Car parking and entry to the visitor centre is free, but there is a small charge for the guided tour. Open Monday to Friday 10 am to 5 pm, with guided tours from 10.30 am to 3.30 pm (3 pm November to February). The visitor centre is signposted from the A153 Sleaford to Horncastle road between Tattershall and neighbouring Coningsby.

☎ *01526 344041*

The George & Dragon

Hagworthingham is a village familiar with boundaries. It is perched on the southern boundary of the Lincolnshire Wolds, part of the county designated as an 'Area of Outstanding Natural Beauty' – which ensures that the landscape on this walk can rival that of a National Park, but without the summer hordes that the designation attracts. The edge of the village is also crossed by the Greenwich Meridian – zero longitude – where east meets west. The walk explores the area to the north of the village and also visits the nature reserve and the country park at Snipe Dales, which is one of the best examples of what this part of the Wolds would have looked like before drainage and arable farming had their effect. As well as the pub, Hagworthingham also has a shop, tearoom and post office.

Distance – 4½ miles (3½ miles for those with dogs)

OS Explorer 273 Lincolnshire Wolds South. GR 346696
The route gives easy walking through undulating countryside. There are some stiles and in places the going can become muddy. A short length of the route runs through a nature reserve where dogs are not allowed – a bypass is described in the walk directions.

Starting point The George & Dragon at Hagworthingham.

How to get there *The pub stands next to the A158 Skegness road, about 5½ miles east of Horncastle. There is limited parking alongside the main road, or if you are using the pub, there is a car park behind the building.*

THE PUB

The **George & Dragon** is a wonderful meeting place for villagers and visitors alike. Welcoming, with low ceilings and a bar that serves Jennings and Marston's, there is a warm conservatory extension and a play area at the back. The George & Dragon has been serving locally-sourced food for many years and has it down to a fine art. There is a Light Bites menu including baguettes, soup, gammon and jacket potatoes. The main menu offers deep-fried prawn torpedo with sweet chilli dip, duck spring rolls with plum sauce dip. It also includes the chef's specials of lamb shank with mint gravy, turkey and gammon pie and mixed grill. There is a good selection for vegetarians.

Open Monday to Friday 12 noon to 3 pm (closed Wednesday afternoon) and 6 pm (5 pm Friday) to 11 pm; Saturday and Sunday 12 noon to 11 pm. Food is served from 12 noon to 2 pm and from 5 pm to 9 pm.
☎ *01507 588255*

Hagworthingham Walk 10

1 Carry on down the track that leads to the pub car park. This is stoned to begin with, but changes to grass at the last house. Follow the waymarks across a field to a stile, continue over a grass field and then turn left along a tarmac bridleway that leads past a pig farm. Shortly after the farm, on a right bend, a footpath sets off to the left – following a walkway of sleepers over boggy ground. The path carries on with a field boundary to the left and approaches a group of isolated buildings.

2 Turn right in front of the house (ignoring a footpath signposted to the left) and, after about 30 yards, turn left at a fingerpost and climb steps to an arable field. Strike off diagonally right, heading towards the low tower of **Ashby Puerorum church**. Cross the next stile and turn left along a field edge to reach a junction of paths marked with a fingerpost, where you turn left

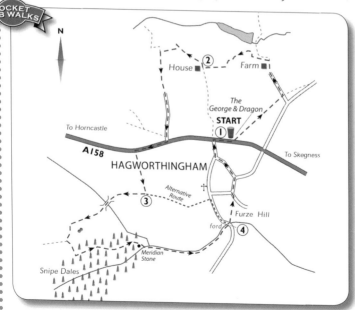

POCKET PUB WALKS

N

House ■ —2— Farm ■

The George & Dragon

START
1

To Horncastle

A158

HAGWORTHINGHAM

To Skegness

Alternative Route

3

Furze Hill

ford

4

Meridian Stone

Snipe Dales

The attractive countryside of the Lincolnshire Wolds

along a track. The route begins to run downhill and after ¼ mile meets the A158. Take care when crossing the road and follow it to the right for about 300 yards before turning left over a stile onto a footpath signposted along a track, which you follow to a path junction where the hedge on the right ends.

3 *For the shorter dog-friendly route*, turn left back to the road in Hagworthingham, where a right turn will lead down and over the ford to rejoin the main walk at point 4.

For the main walk, turn right and follow the track, which soon falls steeply to a bridge before reascending to a gap in the hedge beside a fingerpost. Continue straight ahead, running parallel to a small wood in the valley to your left, until (level with the end of the wood) the path descends steeply through trees, crosses the spring line and enters **Snipe Dales Nature Reserve** at a bridge over a stream. About 100 yards further on, turn left along a grass track signposted as the footpath to **Snipe Dales Country Park**. The track drops to a stream and then climbs to enter woodland, where you should turn left onto a track marked with red waymarks as part of the **Snipe Dales round**. After a few hundred yards, take a path with orange waymarkers that runs off to the left and leads to the **Greenwich Meridian** stone. Beyond this turn left at a pond onto a path with white waymarks, signposted to **Hagworthingham** – the path runs over a stile and through grass fields beside the stream to the road.

4 Cross the road and climb the stile into **Furze Hill Nature Reserve** and almost immediately bear left to cross the stream by a footbridge. Continue uphill over two stiles to a track, where a left turn leads to a road. Continue ahead along **Manor Road** and then bear left into **Bond Hays Lane**. Turn right at the next road junction and walk uphill back to the main road, where a right turn returns you to the **George & Dragon**.

Place of interest nearby

Stockwith Mill, with a working wheel, stands in Tennyson country beside 'The Brook'. There is a Tennyson exhibition, tearoom and licensed restaurant and craft shop. Admission and parking are free. Open: March to September, Tuesday to Sunday from 10.30 am to 6 pm; October 10.30 am to dusk; November and December, Saturday and Sunday only from 10.30 am to dusk. The mill is just 1 mile north of Hagworthingham, beside the road to Brinkhill.
☎ *01507 588221*

11 Goulceby

The Three Horseshoes

Rocky outcrops are few and far between in Lincolnshire, but this walk passes three: the unusual coloured chalk exposed at Red Hill and also two examples of green sandstone, more commonly seen in the walls of local churches. The walk is centred on Goulceby, a small village folded into the curves of the Wolds that stands on a tributary of the River Bain. The walk follows part of the Viking Way long-distance footpath; there are views over the Wolds and of Stenigot Pylon, part of a Second World War radar station and now a listed building. On the way back to the village, there is the chance to visit Red Hill Nature Reserve, the location of an exciting project that is recreating 57 acres of open grassland landscape of the kind that used to dominate the Wolds. Those with an interest in gruesome trivia may also wish to note that Goulceby was the birthplace of the hangman William Marwood,

Distance – 5½ miles

OS Explorer 282 Lincolnshire Wolds North, 273 Lincolnshire Wolds South. GR 253790
A mixture of footpaths, green lanes and minor roads. The surface underfoot is generally good, but there are a few stiles to negotiate. The climb past Stenigot House is steep, but other than this the route is fairly level.

Starting point The Three Horseshoes at Goulceby.

How to get there *Goulceby lies 1½ miles to the west of the A153 Louth road, some 6 miles north of Horncastle. There is parking on the road opposite the pub.*

who invented the somewhat more humane 'long drop' system of execution introduced in 1872.

THE PUB It should come as no great surprise to learn that the **Three Horseshoes** in Shoe Lane started life as a blacksmith's. The interior is welcoming, with low ceilings and weighty beams – and there are two open fires for when the days grow colder. The pub is well known locally for its food, ranging from sandwiches, steaks and salads, to (in the summer months) a full roast Sunday lunch. Outside there is a play area, beer garden and even a small campsite, which makes it a tempting base for exploring other walks in the Wolds.

Opening hours vary, but typical times are Monday to Sunday 12 noon to 3 pm and 7 pm to midnight. In the winter months, the pub is likely to be closed at lunchtimes and only open in the evenings from 7.30 pm. However, groups can be catered for at other times, if advance arrangements are made.
☎ *01507 343610*

1 At the entrance to the car park, turn left down **Shoe Lane** and left again at the road junction. Just beyond the bridge, a footpath leads off left into a grass field. The path bends to the right across the field, before striking off to the left to a kissing gate in the far corner. Beyond, a bridge gives access to a green lane leading to **Top Lane**.

2 Cross the road onto a track – part of the **Viking Way**. Shortly after, a yew tree marks the entrance to the old graveyard – a peaceful haven. Continue past the entrance to the graveyard and through gates onto a track, which leads in about ½ mile through a gate and adjacent stile into a large field.

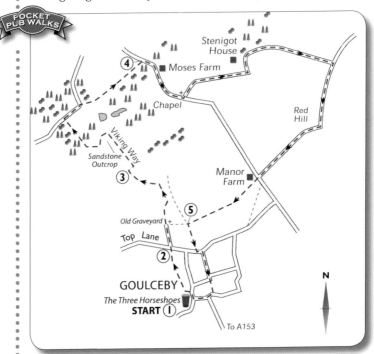

The old graveyard passed at point 2 of the walk

3 Follow the edge of the field to the right and down the hill until, as you approach the far side, the path turns to the left down the valley past a small sandstone outcrop. Skirt round a boggy area beyond and follow the fingerpost to the right to a stile and footbridge that lead into woodland. A hand gate leads out of the trees and the path proceeds along the edge of the wood to reach the road. Turn right here and follow the road until, at a sharp left bend, a signposted bridleway bears off to the right and heads on as a green lane with views to the left of the Stenigot Pylon.

4 At the end of the lane, turn right onto the road, passing **Moses Farm**, and follow it to a small chapel. Take the left turning signposted to Raithby and Louth and start the steady climb past **Stenigot House** to the top of the Wolds. After a mile, at a T-junction, turn right onto the road signposted to Goulceby which leads past **Red Hill Nature Reserve** down to a junction beside

Manor Farm. Cross over the road and go through the gate to follow a waymarked track between buildings until a second gate takes you into the fields beyond. The path continues to be waymarked until you meet another footpath at a signpost.

5 Turn left through a kissing gate and carry on with the hedge on your right. At the next road, turn left and almost immediately right into **Butt Lane**. When the road bends to the right, take a footpath that carries straight ahead over a bridge. This leads you to a road where you turn right, merging with **Main Road**, before you reach the turning on the left into **Shoe Lane** and back to the pub.

Places of interest nearby

There is plenty to see and do in the market town of **Louth** itself, but **St James' church**, with its 295-ft spire (the highest of any ancient parish church in the country) is its crowning glory. In addition to being an active place of worship, the church is open to visitors and has a coffee and gift shop. The late medieval tower can be climbed, for which a small charge is made. As well as regular Sunday and weekday services, the church is open from the first Monday in April until Christmas: Monday to Saturday 10.30 am to 4 pm, and from Christmas until the first Monday of April: Monday, Wednesday, Friday and Saturday 8 am to 12 noon.
☎ 01507 603118

The motor racing circuit at **Cadwell Park** was opened in 1934 and remains one of the most challenging in the country. Cadwell Park is signposted from the A153 Horncastle road, some 4 miles south-west of Louth. There are race meetings throughout the year – further information can be found on the website: www.cadwellpark.org.uk/index.html

12 **Ludborough**

The Livesey Arms

This walk rewards some gentle climbing with enormous views that stretch out to the North Sea from the top of the Lincolnshire Wolds. On the way it passes the site of two deserted villages (there are over 230 in the county), reminders of a time before the rise of sheep farming in the 15th century when communities could survive, if not flourish, in the higher valleys. The route starts in the village of Ludborough, on a broad clay terrace between the Wolds and the sea known as the Middle Marsh, and heads out westward to the tiny, but ancient, church at Wyham before looping round to visit lakes in the remote valley of Cadeby. The tops of the Wolds can be quite exposed at certain times of year, but the Livesey Arms provides a welcoming base for the excursion.

THE PUB

The brick-built **Livesey Arms** provides the chance to relax before or after the walk, listen to the banter of the locals and

Distance – 5 miles

OS Explorer 282 Lincolnshire Wolds North. GR 295955
Good walking on tracks and grass bridleways. There are
two stile crossings.

Starting point The Livesey Arms, Ludborough.

How to get there *Approaching from the A16 Grimsby road,
Ludborough is signposted along the A18 about 5 miles north of
Louth. The Livesey Arms is near the church in the centre of the
village. If you are using the pub, there is a car park at the back.
Alternatively there is limited roadside parking beside the church.*

enjoy a meal in the bright airy restaurant. The bar has a warm
Arts and Crafts feel to it, with a split wood bar and wrought-iron
panels with coats of arms on either side of a wood-burning stove.
Wednesday is home-made 'Pie and Pud' night and at other times
the menu includes a choice of starters, including mushrooms
with Stilton and Parma ham and white bait. The choice of main
courses features fillet of beef with Madeira sauce, roasted duck
in sweet plum sauce and a range of traditional pub grub. There
is a tempting range of desserts. For the thirsty, cask ales include
Black Sheep and Tom Wood, along with a selection of lagers and
other beers, ciders and spirits.

*Open Monday to Wednesday 5.30 pm to 11 pm, Thursday to
Saturday 12 noon to 2 pm (3 pm Saturday) and 5.30 pm to
11 pm, and Sunday 12 noon to 11 pm. The restaurant is open
Tuesday and Wednesday 5.30 pm to 9.30 pm, Thursday to
Saturday 12 noon to 2 pm (3 pm Saturday) and 5.30 pm to
9.30 pm, and Sunday 12 noon to 5 pm. Closed Monday.*
☎ *01472 840993*

Ludborough Walk 12

1 Cross the road from the car park and head left, past the Ludborough service station and then take the first right by the telephone box. At the end of the road bear left, over a stile and onto a grassy footpath that after about 200 yards joins a stone track. The track continues until it bends sharply to the right, next to a plantation – at this point the footpath continues straight ahead, crosses a field and joins the A18.

2 Cross the road with care, turn left and then immediately right onto a bridleway lined with horse chestnuts which forms the impressive drive to **Wyham House**. The track climbs between fields which were once the site of the village of **Wyham** – you can still see the rectangular house plots separated by sunken trackways. Beside the church, take the right-hand track (the other track is marked as private) to reach a junction of bridleways marked with a fingerpost.

3 Turn right at the junction, through a metal bridleway gate and continue along with a hedgerow on your left. There are superb views over the marsh to the sea, with the Grimsby Dock Tower visible in the distance. This was built in 1852 to a design based

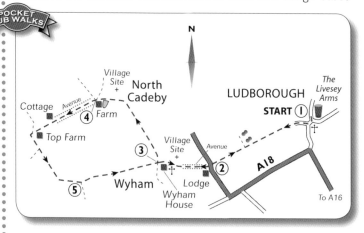

Ludborough church

on the Palazzo Publico in Sienna, Italy. When you come to a gap in the hedge, continue ahead along a grassy swathe to reach a fence at the corner of an area of old grassland – all that is left of the village of **North Cadeby**. Follow the fence downhill to the left and through a gate to pass beside a small lake. The path then begins to rise again, through another gate near farm buildings, and picks up a stone track along a prominent avenue of trees.

4 Ignore a bridleway signposted off to the right and follow the avenue uphill, passing a lonely little cottage, to meet another bridleway at a fingerpost beside a tree, just beyond the buildings of **Top Farm**. Turn left here and where the stone track bends sharply to the right, continue ahead on a waymarked grass path that completes the climb to the top of the Wolds, some 380 ft above sea level. As you turn eastwards and begin the descent you can glimpse Covenham Reservoir in the distance beyond the white houses of Ludborough.

5 At the next surfaced track, turn left and yomp downhill to the junction of bridleways (point 3), from which you reverse the route down the drive, over the A18 and back to the **Livesey Arms**.

Place of interest nearby

A length of the former East Lincolnshire Railway, which used to run between Boston and Grimsby, is being restored by enthusiasts as the **Lincolnshire Wolds Railway** which can claim to be the only standard-gauge steam railway in Lincolnshire open to the public. The station has been rebuilt and there is a museum, picnic site, café and gift shop, as well as the opportunity to see on-going restoration of locomotives and rolling stock. Admission to the site and car parking is free, but a fare is payable for trips along the length of track. The railway is situated on Station Road, a mile east of Ludborough and close to the A16 Grimsby to Louth road. Details of opening times and of steam and diesel days are available on the website: www.lincolnshirewoldsrailway.co.uk/days.html
☎ *01507 363881*

The Red Lion Inn

Drive carefully as you approach Redbourne – the ducks that frequent the small pond close to the Red Lion show no respect for the Green Cross Code. In fact the village takes its name from the reedy stream that the ducks still enjoy, which is why one appears at the top of the village sign on the green. Joined on to the pub is a quaint old fire station that contains an 1830s fire engine. Together, the inn, pond and green form as pleasant a scene as one could hope to find. The walk explores the surprisingly remote countryside to the south of the village, overlooking the Ancholme valley, and passes Redbourne Hall, once a seat of the Dukes of St Albans, descendants of Charles II and Nell Gwyn.

Distance – 6½ miles

OS Explorer 281 Ancholme Valley. GR 971998
Much of the walk is along tracks, but some sections cross arable fields and may at times be muddy. There are no stiles on the route.

Starting point The Red Lion Inn, Redbourne.

How to get there *Redbourne lies on the B1206, just to the east of the A15, 5 miles south of its junction with the M180. There is car parking on the loop of road on which the inn stands.*

THE PUB

The **Red Lion** is a coaching inn, dating from the 17th century. Inside, the main bar is dotted with candlelit tables and a panelled side bar has a welcoming open fire in winter. Towards the rear of the building the large garden room is also used for dining, and there is outside seating to the front and side of the inn. There is a wide choice of food available on the various menu boards arranged around the bar. For light lunchtime snacks you can choose from baguettes or paninis with fillings such as Cajun chicken, apple and Stilton or fig, cranberry and Brie. There is also a choice of larger lunch or evening menus and on Sunday a traditional roast lunch is served, with vegetarian and fish options available. Among the beers on tap are Black Sheep and Shepherd's Delight.

Open every day from 12 noon, with food served all day up to 9 pm.
☎ 01652 648302

Lincolnshire

1 Turn left out of the pub car park and, taking care across the main road, continue into **Vicarage Lane**. At the signpost for the footpath to **Redbourne Hall** turn left and follow the waymarks round the edge of the playing field until, just inside the churchyard, you turn right by a large yew tree. Carry on through a kissing gate and follow the field boundary before the path cuts across the field to join another path on the other side, where you should turn right (still signposted to Redbourne Hall).

2 When you reach the next junction turn left onto a path, marked to Redbourne Heights, that skirts the walled grounds of the Hall. Turn right at the next junction, towards **Sallowrow Drain**, and follow the waymarks as the track bends this way and that and climbs, only a few feet, but enough to give wide views over the Ancholme valley.

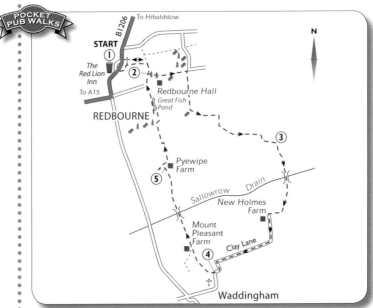

Redbourne's handsome village sign

3 After crossing a deep drain, the track bends sharply to the left, but the public footpath carries straight on, crossing a field to a footbridge marked with fingerposts. More fingerposts mark the line of the path until it meets a track and turns right towards the buildings of **New Holmes Farm**. Turn left in front of the house onto **Clay Lane**. The long straight stretch of Clay Lane comes to an end with a set of zigzags near the edge of **Waddingham**.

4 At the second left bend, turn right onto a signposted footpath that sets off to the right of a field boundary. Follow the waymarks around the field-edge, then as they bear left into the next field and climb towards the buildings of **Mount Pleasant Farm**. At the footpath junction next to the old farm buildings carry on along a track, passing straight on through a metal barrier where the track bends to the left. Go through a gate and over a bridge and then bear to the left to pick up the path that follows a line of electricity poles towards **Pyewipe Farm**.

5 Follow the waymarks to the left around the farm buildings and opposite the houses turn right over a ditch board onto a path that starts by doubling back towards the farm, before bending left and regaining the alignment towards Redbourne. The path carries on past the banks of the **Great Fish Pond** and crosses the drive to **Redbourne Hall** to rejoin the walk at point 2. From here you retrace your steps for a short distance to the pub.

Places of interest nearby

Gainsthorpe is one of the best-preserved examples of a deserted medieval village, identified following aerial photography in 1924. You can still see the grassy humps and hollows where once houses stood and lanes ran. Why was it abandoned – plague or economic change? Local legend has a more colourful explanation – that it was pulled down because 'nobody inhabited there but thieves'. The site is open all year at reasonable times and entry is free. Accessed from a minor road running between the A15, some 3 miles south of the M180 junction, and the B1398.

A traditional four-sailed tower mill built in 1875, **Kirton in Lindsey windmill** is still working and produces eleven different sorts of organic flour; the bread is baked in a wood-fired oven. There is a tearoom and a wholefood shop. Open all year round: Tuesday to Sunday, 10 am to 5 pm, but closed on Monday, except bank holidays. An admission charge applies to the mill. The windmill stands next to the B1398, just to the north of Kirton and 2 miles to the west of the A15.
☎ *01652 640177*

14 Barnetby le Wold

The Railway Inn

This walk climbs to visit the tops of the Wolds, here some 300 ft high. It has a transport theme: the excursion starts next to a railway and on the way it gives views of the tops of the towers of the Humber Bridge and the runways of Humberside International Airport. The way back is along a long-distance footpath – a gentle low-level section of the Viking Way, as it approaches the end of its 147-mile journey from Rutland to the banks of the Humber. The railway reached Barnetby in 1848 and led to its development as a major junction; the village still has an operating station, which makes this the only walk in this book that can be approached by train.

Lincolnshire

Distance – 6 miles

OS Explorer 281 Ancholme Valley. GR 055101
Easy walking on green lanes and a return along field-edge paths following the Viking Way. There are some stiles. The tops of the Wolds can feel exposed in poor weather.

Starting point The Railway Inn in Barnetby le Wold.

How to get there *The village of Barnetby lies some 9 miles south of the Humber Bridge, just south of junction 5 of the M180. Approaching from the motorway, the Railway Inn is on the edge of the village just before the railway bridge. Walkers should check with the landlord if planning to use the pub car park, but there is also roadside parking.*

THE PUB The **Railway Inn** is a comfortable local pub where railway enthusiasts will feel at home – the walls are decked with reminders of Barnetby's railway heritage and there are memorabilia from around the rest of Britain as well. Among the range of beers served are John Smith's and Tetley's. The Railway also provides a choice of traditional pub fare at reasonable prices, including gammon, a variety of steaks, fish and chips, scampi and Lincolnshire sausage and egg. There is a selection of lighter meals, including jacket potatoes, while on Sunday they serve a traditional roast lunch.

Open Monday to Friday from 2 pm to 11 pm, Saturday 12 noon to 4 pm and 7 pm to 11 pm, and Sunday 12 noon to 4 pm and 7 pm to 10.30 pm. Food is served every day at lunchtime and in the evenings, except Monday, but it is best to check beforehand as precise times can vary.
☎ *01652 688284*

1 Turn under the railway bridge and along **Victoria Road** towards the centre of the village. After about ¼ mile, turn right into **Walkers Close** and pass between barriers into a footpath that leads straight through to **St Barnabas Road** next to the school. Turn right along the road and soon after cross over by the bus shelter and to enter a signposted footpath along **Smithy Lane**.

2 The path leads over a stile and into a grass field. Walk uphill across the field, trending to the left, to reach a second stile next to a gate, where you can stop to admire the view over Barnetby behind you. The path continues, now with a hedge on the right, to reach a road. Turn left towards the old windmill and almost immediately right beside a fingerpost, over two stiles onto a long undulating path that after ½ mile brings you out on a minor road high on the Wolds.

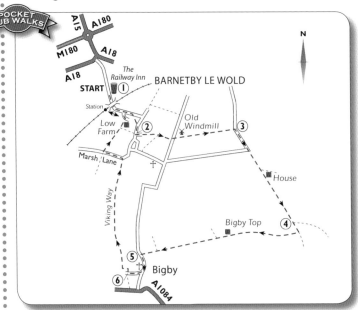

Bigby church

3 Follow the road to the right until it bends sharply to the right beside a derelict building. Carry straight on at this point, onto a surfaced bridleway leading towards **Wold Farm**. In ¼ mile, when the tarmac ends next to a house, go straight ahead as the bridleway becomes a broad hedged green lane rising and falling with the contours of the Wolds. Just over the brow of a hill, where the lane turns abruptly to the left, carry on onto a narrower unhedged grass track, still signposted as a bridleway.

4 Follow this track for just a couple of hundred yards before it turns sharply to the right at a signposted junction with another

bridleway. The track narrows down now and climbs gently past the farm buildings of **Bigby Top** to reach the summit of our walk. Behind are the runways of Humberside International Airport, while away to the north the towers of the Humber Bridge are visible on a clear day. Keep to the public bridleway, ignoring other tracks running off to the right, and descend quite steeply towards the end, to reach the main road.

5 Cross the road with care and follow the verge to the left for a few yards until a surfaced footway starts at the entrance to the village of **Bigby**. Just past the church take the minor road off to the right, which leads downhill to join the **Viking Way** – waymarked with its distinctive horned-helmet logo.

6 Follow the **Viking Way** to the right as it leads back towards **Barnetby** along a well-signposted series of field-edge paths and tracks. At **Marsh Lane**, turn left along the road for 400 yards and then right onto a bridleway that runs past the buildings of Low Farm to **St Mary's Avenue**, where a left turn leads back to **Victoria Road**. Another left turn here takes you back to the pub.

Places of interest nearby

Elsham Hall Gardens and Country Park is an attraction with an appeal that extends beyond keen gardeners. It includes an arboretum, sensory garden, wild butterfly garden and, for younger visitors, an animal farm and adventure playground. There are cafés and a restaurant on site. Open weekends from Easter Saturday to the end of September (and every day during school holidays) from 11 am to 5 pm. Elsham is situated on the B1206, just two miles north-west of the M180/A180 interchange (junction 5 on the M180).
☎ 01652 688698 www.elshamhall.co.uk

The Steer Arms

The final walk in this book visits the Isle of Axholme. The Isle has an aura of mystery about it. It is the only part of Lincolnshire to lie beyond the Trent and in the past was cut off from surrounding counties by the marshy surrounds of the rivers Don, Trent and Idle – a true inland island that feels remote to this day. This short walk leads around Belton, which holds a central position in the string of Axholme villages, and follows the line of one of the county's most shortlived railways – the Isle of Axholme Joint Railway, which was completed in 1909 and closed in the 1930s. In 1626 Axholme became the site of the first of the large-scale drainage schemes that went on to change the appearance of Lincolnshire when Charles I agreed that Cornelius Vermuyden could seek to make the area 'fit for tillage and pasture', in exchange for one third of the land drained. The

Distance – 3 miles

OS Explorer 280 Isle of Axholme. GR 785061
A stile-free route around the edge of the village of Belton, using footpaths and an old railway line.

Starting point The Steer Arms in Belton.

How to get there *Belton lies just a mile to the south of the M180 on the A161 Goole to Gainsborough road. The Steer Arms is among the last buildings on the southern edge of the village, just at the entrance to Belgrave Close. Walkers may use the pub car park with permission and there is also some roadside parking.*

process led to the diversion of the rivers Don and Idle and was violently opposed by those who relied on the fenland for their livelihoods.

THE PUB The **Steer Arms** is a very friendly country pub that is well known locally for the range and quality of the food it serves. The main bar is spacious and decorated with old photographs of the village – some showing the railway in its heyday. At one end is an open fireplace, with comfortable seating around it, and there is a conservatory style extension for additional dining space. The bar serves Tetley's and John Smith's beer, while around on a number of boards are details of the various menus. For lunchtime snacks there is a range of reasonably priced hot and cold sandwiches, which are served with chips and salad. There are separate fish and steak menus and one for 'sizzling dishes' that includes fajitas and Cajun sizzling salad. There are seven choices on the vegetarian menu and a sweet selection that demands further investigation. For sunny days, there is a large beer garden with children's play equipment.

Open 11 am to 11 pm every day. Food served every day from
12 noon to 2 pm and 5 pm to 9 pm.
☎ *01427 872424*

1 From the pub car park, turn left, continue down **Belgrave Close**
and then bear left to meet the old railway. Turn right, pass
through barriers and follow the line until you drop down to the
A161. Take care when crossing the road and enter a picnic site.

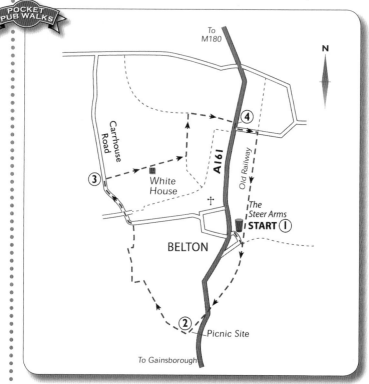

Looking towards Belton church

Carry on ahead, passing to the right of the car park, to a point (marked with a fingerpost) where a public footpath crosses the railway line.

2 Turn right onto a stone track, soon narrowing to a path that follows the edge of the fields northwards for about ½ mile before emerging onto **Carrhouse Road**. Carry on straight ahead along the road, ignoring the first footpath off to the right, and 150 yards after the last house in the hamlet, turn right onto a signposted footpath.

3 Follow the track, passing the **White House**, and shortly after, where it bends to the right, take a footpath that carries straight on and leads to a junction with a grass track where you turn left. After a few hundred yards this path ends at a stone track, which you must follow to the right back to the A161.

4 Take care crossing the main road and then turn right, and almost immediately left, into **Jeffrey Lane**. Walk down the road

until you meet the old railway line once more (signposted as a bridleway). Turn right, passing a play area, and follow the line for ½ mile back to the Belgrave Close junction, where a final right turn will take you back to the **Steer Arms**.

Places of interest nearby

Epworth Old Rectory was the childhood home of John and Charles Wesley, and so played its part in the birth of Methodism. The house is now owned by the Methodist Church and is open to the public, with a guided tour, garden and shop. Open from the beginning of March to the end of October (including bank holidays): March, April and October, Monday to Saturday 10 am to 12 noon and 2 pm to 4 pm, Sunday 2 pm to 4 pm; May to September, Monday to Saturday 10 am to 4.30 pm, Sunday 2 pm to 4.30 pm. There is limited parking. The Old Rectory stands in Epworth, which is on the A161 Goole road, about 12 miles north of Gainsborough. Once in the town, follow the brown museum or Old Rectory signs.
☎ *01427 872268*

The magnificent medieval manor of **Gainsborough Old Hall** was once the home of the Burgh family, who counted Richard III and Henry VIII among their guests. The centrepiece of the building is the Great Hall with its splendid timber roof, but the kitchens remain virtually unchanged since they were built and there are extensive views of the Trent from the tower. There is also a tearoom and gift shop. Open from Monday to Saturday all year from 10 am to 5 pm and also from Easter to the end of October on Sunday afternoons from 1 pm until 4.30 pm. The Old Hall is located in the centre of Gainsborough and is easy to find following the brown tourist signs.
☎ *01427 612669*